50 Homemade Martini Recipes

(50 Homemade Martini Recipes - Volume 1)

Linda Davis

Content

50 Awesome Martini Recipes

***

1. Apple Cider Honey Jack Martini

Serving: Makes 1 martini | Prep: | Cook: | Ready in:

Ingredients

- 2 ounces Jack Daniel's Tennessee Honey Whiskey Liqueur
- 1 ounce unfiltered apple cider
- 1/2 ounce freshly squeezed lemon juice
- ground cinnamon
- sliced apple for garnish

Direction

- Combine Honey Jack, lemon, and cider in a shaker with a pinch of cinnamon. Add ice and shake.
- Rim the martini glass with a mixture of ground cinnamon & granulated sugar, then garnish with apple slices.

2. Apple Martini

Serving: Makes 2 | Prep: 0hours5mins | Cook: 0hours30mins | Ready in:

Ingredients

- 4 Fuji apples, cut in thin slices with skin and seeds
- 2 cups filtered water
- 3 cinnamon sticks
- 1/4 teaspoon ginger

- 1 cup honey
- 2 ounces vodka
- 2 ounces pure pressed apple juice
- 2 ounces apple infusion
- 1-2 cups ice cubes

Direction

- To make the apple infusion, place sliced apples in a medium stock pot.
- Add the water, cinnamon sticks, ginger, and honey.
- Bring to a boil, reduce heat to a light boil, and cook 5 minutes.
- Remove from heat, and let sit for 30 minutes.
- To make the martinis: Use a shaker, fill with ice cubes, add the vodka, apple juice, and apple infusion, and shake vigorously for 10 seconds.
- Dip the rim of frozen martini glasses in vodka or water, then in cinnamon sugar mixture.
- Pour into the martini glasses, garnish with apple slice and cinnamon stick if desired.

3. Basil Martini

Serving: Serves 2 | Prep: | Cook: | Ready in:

Ingredients

- 4 shots Kettle One Citron Vodka
- 5 shots Simple Syrup
- 3 handfuls Fresh Basil
- 2 sprigs Basil
- 1 Lime
- Ice
- 5 shots Sparkling water

Direction

- Add basil and simple syrup to a shaker.
- Muddle basil.
- Add vodka.

- Squeeze all the juice from the lime into the shaker. Roll the lime on the counter before cutting to get the most juice out of it!
- Add sparkling water.
- Add ice.
- Shake vigorously and pour into glasses.
- Garnish with a sprig of basil and a straw.

4. Blackberry Martini

Serving: Serves 1 | Prep: | Cook: |Ready in:

Ingredients

- For the Blackberry Jam:
- 2 tablespoons sugar
- 1 cup blackberries
- For the Blackberry Martini:
- 2 ounces gin (use a gin that's not perfumey or intense, like Beefeater or Tanqueray)
- 1/4 ounce Grand Marnier (or 1/2 ounce if you want a sweeter drink)
- 2 teaspoons fresh lime juice
- 1 tablespoon blackberry jam (or a bit less if you want a tarter drink)
- 3 blackberries
- 1 basil leaf

Direction

- For the Blackberry Jam:
- Place 2 tablespoons of sugar in the bottom of a heavy-bottomed saucepan. Add a splash of water. Swirl it around on medium heat until all the sugar is moist. Cook until the sugar just starts to caramelize (you'll see a bit of caramel color and smell a hint of burning sugar).
- Take off the heat and carefully pour in 1 cup of blackberries. Stir. The mixture will seize up. Don't panic. Put back on medium heat and keep stirring for about 3 minutes. It's ready when the berries have released their juices and it looks like jam.

- Cool. Pass through a fine strainer. Use the jam in your blackberry martini or have it on toast (it will keep for a few days in the fridge).
- For the Blackberry Martini:
- Chill a martini glass. Place a large handful of ice in a cocktail shaker or a large glass. Add the gin, Grand Marnier, lime juice, and blackberry jam. Stir vigorously with a cocktail spoon (or shake away if that's your thing).
- Strain into the chilled glass. Add 3 blackberries. Rub a bruised basil leaf along the rim of the glass. Float leaf on top. Drink.

5. Butternut Sage Martini

Serving: Serves one | Prep: | Cook: |Ready in:

Ingredients

- For butternut-sage simple syrup
- 1/2 cup butternut liquid, drained from a cooked, mashed butternut squash (see Butternut-Sage Scones recipe), or water
- 1/2 cup turbinado sugar
- 1/4 cup fresh sage leaves
- For the maple-sage sugared walnuts and the butternut-sage martini
- 1 cup raw walnuts, halves and pieces
- 1 tablespoon chopped fresh sage
- 1 tablespoon egg whites
- 2 tablespoons maple syrup
- 1 tablespoon light brown sugar
- fresh sage leaf – one large, one small
- 1/4 ounce Nocello (walnut liqueur)
- 2 ounces vodka
- 3/4 ounce butternut-sage syrup, plus more for rimming glass
- 1 tablespoon finely crushed maple sugared walnuts

Direction

- For butternut-sage simple syrup
- Place all ingredients in a small saucepan over medium-low heat. Stir until sugar dissolves

and mixture starts to steam. Remove from heat, let cool while the sage infuses the syrup.

- When cool, strain syrup into a jar. Keeps for a week in the refrigerator.
- For the maple-sage sugared walnuts and the butternut-sage martini
- FOR THE MAPLE SUGARED WALNUTS: Preheat oven to 300 degrees F. Prepare a parchment-lined cookie sheet. Place walnuts and chopped sage in a small mixing bowl. Mix egg white and maple syrup in a small cup. Add to walnuts and stir well. Sprinkle the brown sugar over and toss to coat nuts completely. Spill walnuts onto cookie sheet, and spread out in one layer.
- Bake for 15 - 20 minutes, stirring a few times, until nuts are nicely toasted. Slide parchment off of hot cookie sheet onto a cooling rack and cool completely. Store in an airtight container.
- Finely crush a small amount of nuts equal to about a tablespoon. I use my mortar and pestle. Reserve the rest of the walnuts for another use.
- Alternatively, skip the maple sugared walnuts and simply rim the glass in granulated maple sugar.
- FOR THE BUTTERNUT-SAGE MARTINI: Rub inside of martini glass, as well as outer edge, with large sage leaf.
- Place 1 tablespoon butternut-sage syrup in a flat plate. Dip rim of glass in syrup, turning edge of glass all the way around.
- Place crushed maple sugared walnuts, or granulated maple sugar, in a flat plate. Dip wet rim of glass into the mixture, turning edge of glass all the way around.
- In a cocktail shaker filled 2/3 with ice cubes, add Nocello, vodka and butternut-sage syrup. Shake. Pour into prepared glass. Garnish with small sage leaf.
- Cin cin!

Serving: Serves 4 | Prep: | Cook: | Ready in:

Ingredients

- 3/4 pound Turkey suasage
- 3 pieces Boneless skinless chicken breast
- 30 ounces Diced tomatoes
- 15 pieces Green olives, halved
- 1/8 cup Vermouth
- 1 teaspoon Chopped garlic
- 2 tablespoons Fresh parsley
- Thyme
- Oregano
- Pinch of crushed red pepper
- 1 tablespoon Olive oil

Direction

- Heat oil in large pan
- Add sausage and cook until halfway done, flip sausage
- Add chicken until meat is cooked, remove from pan and cut into small pieces
- Lightly brown garlic in pan
- Add vermouth to deglaze pan
- Add remaining ingredients and simmer 10-15 minutes. Add flour for thicker sauce
- Return sausage and chicken to pan and simmer 10 minutes. Serve with pasta.

7. Chicken Martini

Serving: Serves 6 | Prep: | Cook: | Ready in:

Ingredients

- 1 pound boneless, skinless chicken breasts
- 1 pound angel hair pasta
- 1 cup onion, diced
- 3 tablespoons garlic, minced
- 3 tablespoons Worchestershire
- 2 tablespoons Lemonpepper seasoning
- 14 ounces baby artichokes, chopped

- 1 handful Sicilian green olives, pitted and NOT stuffed
- 2 tablespoons olive juice from jar
- 1 cup chicken broth
- 1 cup white wine
- 2 tablespoons gin
- 2 tablespoons lemon juice
- 16 ounces petite diced tomatoes
- 4 tablespoons olive oil

Direction

- Spread the chicken pieces into one layer on a big plate or prep area. Stab with a fork several times, then sprinkle on the Worcestershire followed by a few generous shakes of the lemon pepper.
- Cook pasta according to package directions.
- Heat about 1 tbsp. of olive oil in a large sauté pan over medium-high heat. Throw in the chicken when the oil is hot. Let it brown for about a minute or two, then toss. Turn it, browning the other sides and continue cooking until browned and done - about 6 minutes or so. Move to a plate and cover with foil. Do not rinse the pan...we need those little brown bits!
- Add another tbsp. of olive oil to the pan, and then the garlic and onions. Stir until you can smell the garlic and then add the artichokes through parmesan. Bring to a slow boil, then reduce heat to medium-low and cover. Simmer, and stir occasionally, for about 20 minutes.
- Add the chicken to the sauce and simmer about another one or two minutes, then remove from heat. Toss with the pasta and serve.

8. Citrus And Olive Martini

Serving: Serves 2 | Prep: | Cook: | Ready in:

Ingredients

- 2 ounces your favorite plain vodka
- 2 ounces your favorite gin
- 2 strips of thin lemon peel
- 4 large, pimento-stuffed olives
- 1/2 capful of dry, white vermouth
- 1 cup ice

Direction

- Mix gin, vodka and vermouth in a cocktail shaker with ice. Shake hard and quickly.
- Strain and pour into 2 chilled martini glasses).
- Garnish each glass with a lemon twist and 2 olives (on a toothpick
- Take a sip, enjoy, and know that life is good.

9. Cucumber Martini

Serving: Makes one martini | Prep: | Cook: | Ready in:

Ingredients

- 2 ounces Vodka
- 1/4 ounce Fresh Lemon Juice
- 2 slices cucumber about 1/8" thick
- 3 Leaves of Fresh Mint
- 1/2 ounce Simple Syrup (Sugar Syrup)
- 1/2 cup Ice

Direction

- Muddle mint and a cucumber slice in a cocktail shaker.
- Add ice, vodka, lemon juice, simple syrup, and shake vigorously.
- Strain into a chilled martini or cocktail glass.
- Garnish with a slice of cucumber and a fresh mint sprig.

10. ELECTRIC LADY MARTINI
A Lucid Dreamer

Serving: Serves 1 | Prep: | Cook: | Ready in:

Ingredients

- 2 ounces *Electric Lady Earl Tea, sweetened and chilled
- 3 ounces Vodka
- 1 tablespoon Vermouth
- 2 Pimiento olives speared "up", 1/4" apart on top of glass

Direction

- *Brew I cup, (8-10 ozs.) ELECTRIC LADY EARL TEA, 1-2 level tsp. sugar, chill. Makes 3-4 drinks.
- Shake tea, vodka and vermouth with ice and strain into chilled martini glass. Add olives.

11. Floating Start Martini

Serving: Makes 1 cocktail | Prep: | Cook: | Ready in:

Ingredients

- 2 ounces bourbon
- 2 ounces apple cider
- 1 drop juice from a lime wedge
- 1 apple
- 1 clove star anise

Direction

- Prepare Garnish: slice apple thinly across the apple to reveal the star shaped center. Place in a bowl of ice water & juice from half a lime. This preserves the white of the apple.
- In a cocktail shaker combine the Bourbon, Apple Cider, Pomegranate Liquer and a squeeze of lime wedge over ice. Shake shake shake until mixed.
- Pour into martini glasses, float in a slice of apple and a clove of star anise. Enjoy!

12. Four Ingredient Strawberry Martini

Serving: Makes 2 5 oz martinis | Prep: | Cook: | Ready in:

Ingredients

- 1/2 cup Strawberries, halved, greens removed
- 1 tablespoon sugar
- 1/2 juice of a lemon
- 5 ounces your favorite vodka (I used Kettle One)

Direction

- 1. Add the strawberries, sugar and lemon juice to the bowl of a food processor or blender.
- 2. Blend until the fruit is completely pureed and liquid. You can strain into a separate bowl if you do not like the seeds (or if you use a different kind of fruit that has skin such as grapes or figs)
- 3. Combine the fruit juice and vodka into a drink shaker with a few ice cubes and shake for 30 seconds until cold and well combined.
- 4. Pour into your favorite martini glass (or a high ball glass if you are like Adam and cannot drink out of a martini glass without spilling).
- You can completely swap out the strawberries in this drink and go with grapes, figs, clementine, berries, whatever your little heart desires.

13. Gin Martini

Serving: Makes 1 | Prep: 0hours0mins | Cook: 0hours5mins | Ready in:

Ingredients

- 2 ounces gin

- 1 ounce vermouth
- Ice
- Green olive or lemon twist

Direction

- Pour gin and vermouth into a shaker filled partway with ice.
- Stir vigorously with a long-handled cocktail spoon for at least 30 seconds.
- Strain liquid into a chilled martini glass. Garnish.

14. Grapefruit Martini

Serving: Serves 1 | Prep: | Cook: |Ready in:

Ingredients

- 3 ounces Freshly squeezed grapefruit juice
- 1 1/2 ounces Vodka
- 1/2 ounce Triple Sec
- 1/4 teaspoon Simple Syrup
- 1 Grapefruit peel strip

Direction

- Chill a martini glass by filling it with ice. Rub the glass rim with the peel of a grapefruit. Dip in sugar if desired.
- In a shaker, combine all drink ingredients. Pour ice from glass into shaker with drink ingredients. Replace lid and shake until chilled. Strain liquid into the cold glass and top with grapefruit peel garnish.
- Please note that if the grapefruit is very tart, you can add additional simple syrup to get the desired sweetness.

15. Grilled Martini Pizza And A Party

Serving: Makes 4 medium dough rounds | Prep: | Cook: | Ready in:

Ingredients

- DOUGH & PIZZA TOPPINGS
- 2 ½ cups unbleached all-purpose flour
- 2 teaspoons rapid rise yeast
- 1 teaspoon sea salt
- 1/2 tablespoon honey or agave
- 1 ¾ tablespoon olive oil - plus more on hand to oil the dough balls
- 7 oz room temperature water
- Smoky Balsamic BBQ sauce (recipe below)
- Martini olives – sliced
- Mozzarella – thin sliced or shredded (fresh or packaged)
- An array of fresh sliced garden vegetables
- Optional – Blue Sapphire Martini(s)
- Smoky Balsamic BBQ Sauce
- 1 tablespoon butter
- 1/4 cup brown sugar (I sometimes use honey or agave)
- 2 teaspoons granulated onion powder
- 3 tablespoons dark balsamic vinegar
- 3 tablespoons molasses
- 1-1/2 teaspoon liquid smoke
- 1/8 teaspoon, a pinch, sea salt
- 1/8 teaspoon, a pinch, ground allspice
- 15 oz can tomato sauce
- Optional – Tabasco to taste

Direction

- DOUGH & PIZZA TOPPINGS
- Place all dry dough ingredients in an electric stand mixer with dough hook. Turn the mixer on to lowest speed and slowly stream in the combined wet ingredients.
- Mix on low for 3 minutes or until the dough forms a ball that clears the sides and bottom of the bowl.
- Let the dough rest, covered, for 15 minutes. Mix again on medium low for 5 minutes,

stopping half way to gather dough into a ball, if needed. Mix until the dough is smooth and elastic.

- Divide dough into 4 equal pieces, form each into a ball - this dough is very easy to work with.
- Place each dough ball inside its own Ziploc bag and drizzle in 1 teaspoon of olive oil, covering all sides of the ball. Seal bags and let sit at room temperature for 30 minutes.
- Refrigerate 3 hours to overnight. Let the dough sit at room temperature for a couple hours before working with it.
- READY TO GRILL: Flatten each ball - needs a little flour for this, I like using Wondra. Stack the rounds on top of each other with parchment paper in-between.
- Quickly grill the dough on both sides over high heat, just until starting to bubble, then place the hot rounds on a rack.
- Have each guest dress one up, pretty, fitting for a party, with toppings of choice.
- Place back onto the grill over indirect heat for cheese melting and crisping.
- Smoky Balsamic BBQ Sauce
- In a sauce pan melt the butter, browning it a bit.
- Add the sugar, onion powder, vinegar, molasses, liquid smoke, salt and allspice. Heat ingredients until they start to bubble, stir in tomato sauce and simmer, covered, for an hour.
- Stir in Tabasco sauce to taste, optional.

16. Key Lime Martini

Serving: Serves 1 | Prep: | Cook: |Ready in:

Ingredients

- 2 ounces Vanilla Rum
- 1.5 ounces Pineapple Juice
- 1.5 ounces Simple Lime Syrup
- Lime wedge for serving

- Ice

Direction

- Add all of your ingredients (besides the lime wedge) in your cocktail shaker.
- Shake it like you're really mad at it.
- Pour into martini glass (or just drink straight from the shaker- no judgment here). Your end result after shaking should be a light, sweet, tangy, frothy glass of goodness.

17. Key Lime Pie Martini

Serving: Makes 1 drink | Prep: | Cook: |Ready in:

Ingredients

- Homemade Vanilla Vodka
- 1 liter High Quality Vodka
- 12 pieces Madagascar Vanilla Beans
- Key Lime Pie Martini
- 1 shot Homemade Vanilla Vodka
- 1 shot Vanilla Cream Liquor (Santa Clara Rompope)
- 1 shot Key Lime Juice (fresh squeezed or bottled)
- 1 shot Milk (whole or 2%)
- 1 packet Stevia Sweetner
- 1/2 cup crushed ice

Direction

- Slit the vanilla beans lengthwise. Place the slit vanilla beans in the bottle of vodka. Reseal. Store in a cool dark place for one month prior to pouring. Note: I mark the bottom of the bottle with the date made.
- In a cocktail shaker, place the crushed ice. Add the remaining ingredients. Shake vigorously for 60 seconds. Strain into a martini or large wine glass. Serve immediately. *Optional: sugar the rim of the glass with a rub of lime juice - from a cut wedge of lime - and a dip into confectioner's sugar.

18. LVOV Lemon Drop Martini

Serving: Serves 1 | Prep: 0hours5mins | Cook: 0hours0mins | Ready in:

Ingredients

- 1½ oz. lvov vodka cups LVOV vodka
- ¾ oz. lemon juice ounces lemon juice
- ¼ oz. simple syrup ounces simple syrup
- 1½ cup ice cubes cups ice cubes
- twist of Lime

Direction

- Directions: Fill a shaker with ice. Pour in vodka, lemon juice, and simple syrup and shake well. Strain into a chilled martini glass. Garnish with lemon peel.

19. Lemony Vodka Martini

Serving: Serves 1 | Prep: | Cook: | Ready in:

Ingredients

- 2 ounces KetelOne Vodka
- 1/2 ounce Limoncello Liquor chilled icy cold
- 1 tablespoon lime juice
- 1 sprig 2 or 3 inch sprig of savory

Direction

- In a shaker add ice, vodka, limoncello and lime juice. Shake well.
- Pour into a chilled martini glass. Add a 3 inch sprig of savory and serve.

20. Luis Buñuel Dry Martini

Serving: Makes 1 drink | Prep: | Cook: | Ready in:

Ingredients

- 2.5 ounces Gin
- .5 ounces Dry vermouth
- 2 dashes angostura bitters

Direction

- Fill a mixing glass with ice. Add the vermouth and bitters. Stir and then strain out and discard the excess liquid.
- Add the gin and stir until well-chilled.
- Strain into a chilled cocktail glass.

21. MYSTICEARL MARTINI A Little Dirty And Mystical

Serving: Serves 1 | Prep: | Cook: | Ready in:

Ingredients

- 2 ounces *Mysticearl Tea, sweetened and chilled
- 3 ounces Gin
- 1 tablespoon Vermouth
- 2 Pimiento olives floating

Direction

- Brew I cup, (8-10 oz.) MYSTICEARL TEA, 1-2 level tsp. sugar, chill. Makes 4 drinks.
- Shake tea, gin and vermouth with ice and strain into chilled martini glass. Add olives.

22. Mint Pineapple Martini

Serving: Makes 1 drink | Prep: | Cook: | Ready in:

Ingredients

- 1/4 cup Sweet fresh pineapple
- 3 sprigs Fresh mint
- 3 ounces Gin
- 1/2 ounce Vermouth

Direction

- Muddle the pineapple in a shaker or tall glass for a minute or so to release all the juice.
- Take the leaves off of two mint sprigs so that you have 8-10 leaves (you can't really have too many). Put them in the shaker and muddle on top of the pineapple for another minute so that the mint oils mix into the pineapple juice.
- Add ice to the mixer. Then add the gin and vermouth. Shake for 15 seconds to mix well and chill. Strain into a martini glass. There will be bits of mint unless you use a fine mesh strainer.
- Garnish with the remaining mint sprig.
- Variation: for a Mint Pineapple G&T, omit the vermouth and strain the shaker mix into an ice- filled glass. Top up with tonic to taste and garnish with the mint.

23. Mouthwatering Watermelon Martini

Serving: Serves as many as you need | Prep: | Cook: | Ready in:

Ingredients

- 1 choice watermelon cut into ice-cube size pieces
- 1 bunch fresh mint leaves
- Good quality vodka of your choice
- vermouth (optional)
- 1 teaspoon lime zest

Direction

- Cut your watermelon in half and proceed to chop it into bite size cubes. Remove any seeds.

- Place cubes in a zip-lock bag loosely and freeze.
- When guests are ready, use per martini: 4/5 cubes of the watermelon, 1 fresh mint leaf, 1 1/2 oz. of vodka, one ice cube, vermouth if you need/like it (less is more) and a pinch of lime zest.
- Blend all together quickly so it is slushy. Decorate with a mint leaf, small slice of lime or a flower and a straw. Serve in a chilled martini glass.

24. Muddied Meyer Martini

Serving: Serves 2 | Prep: | Cook: | Ready in:

Ingredients

- The Meyer-infused Vodka
- 4 (or more) Meyer lemons, cut into chunks, peel and all
- A fifth of decent vodka
- The Martini
- 6 ounces of the lemon vodka
- 1 ounce olive juice (Oliver's Twist, Dirty Tony's, Bevmo, etc). In a pinch, you can use the brine from a bottle of top-quality Spanish green olives
- 1 ounce dry vermouth
- 4-6 Spanish green olives, speared on a toothpick

Direction

- The Meyer-infused Vodka
- Put the chunks of Meyer lemon in a quart-sized (or larger) wide-mouthed glass jar, fill with vodka, and put in the refrigerator for a couple of days. Use any leftover vodka to make penne with vodka sauce or Bloody Mary's or something.
- The Martini
- Strain vodka into a shaker half-filled with cracked ice, add olive juice and vermouth. Shake briskly for 30 seconds or so, and strain

into a well-chilled cocktail glass. Garnish with the speared olives.

25. My Blue Heaven Martinis

Serving: Makes 1 martini | Prep: | Cook: | Ready in:

Ingredients

- 2 ounces Vodka
- 1 ounce Blue Curacao Liqueur
- 1/2 ounce Lemon juice
- 1 Lemon wedge
- 2 tablespoons Wilton Sprinkles Sapphire blue sugar
- 1 Lemon twists
- 6 ice cubes

Direction

- Into a cocktail shaker, pour the Vodka, Curacao and Lemon Juice.
- Add ice. Shake well.
- Rub the rim of the martini glass with the wedge of lemon. Dip rim of glass in blue sugar.
- Strain and pour the contents of the cocktail shaker into a martini glass. Garnish with lemon twists.

26. Pear Martini Crisp

Serving: Makes 9-inch pan | Prep: | Cook: | Ready in:

Ingredients

- Pear mix
- 2 1/2 cups peeled, cored, and sliced fresh pears (4-5 large pears)
- 1/3 cup pear or vanilla vodka
- 1 teaspoon lemon juice
- 2 teaspoons cinnamon
- 1/4 teaspoon nutmeg

- 1/4 cup sugar
- Topping
- 1/3 cup butter
- 2/3 cup flour
- 2/3 cup chopped walnuts
- 1/2 cup brown sugar

Direction

- Preheat oven to 350 degrees Fahrenheit. Spray an 8-inch round cake pan or 9-inch pie plate with non-stick cooking spray; set aside.
- In a medium bowl, stir together vodka, lemon juice, cinnamon, nutmeg and sugar. Add pears and toss until fruit is completely glazed. Pour mixture into prepared pan; set aside.
- Topping: In a medium microwave-safe bowl, melt the butter. Stir in flour, walnuts and sugar until well combined and crumbly. Sprinkle mixture evenly over pears.
- Bake for 35-40 minutes or until topping is golden brown and bubbly. Remove from oven and let cool. To serve, spoon pear crisp into individual serving bowls. Top with vanilla ice cream and whipped cream. Sprinkle lightly with cinnamon, if desired.

27. Pear Vodka Martini

Serving: Makes 1 | Prep: 0hours5mins | Cook: 0hours0mins | Ready in:

Ingredients

- 4 tablespoons Pear Vodka
- 3 tablespoons Pear Nectar
- 2 tablespoons Simple Syrup
- 1 tablespoon Fresh Lemon Juice
- 1 handful Ice

Direction

- Fill a cocktail shaker half way full with ice and place your martini glass in the freezer for a quick chill.

- Combine all of the ingredients into the shaker and shake vigorously to combine, about 30 seconds.
- Pour into your already chilled glass. Enjoy!

28. Perfect And Pretty Pom Martini

Serving: Makes 2 cocktails | Prep: | Cook: | Ready in:

Ingredients

- 1 Lg Pomegranate squeezed to yield 1/2 C juice
- 1/2 Grapefruit, squeezed to yield 1/4C juice
- 1 tablespoon Ginger simple syrup or straight simple syrup
- 1/2 Lime, squeezed for juice
- 2-3 sprigs Mint + tips for garnish
- 3 ounces Vodka - or more

Direction

- Add the ingredients to a shaker filled with ice. Shake and strain into chilled martini glasses. Garnish with mint leaves

29. Pickle Brine Martini

Serving: Makes 1 (big!) martini | Prep: 0hours0mins | Cook: 0hours0mins | Ready in:

Ingredients

- 2 1/4 ounces gin
- 1 1/2 ounces dry vermouth
- 1/2 to 3/4 ounces sour pickle brine, to taste
- 1 cornichon

Direction

- Fill a shaker with glass. Add the gin, vermouth, and pickle brine. Shake until very,

very cold. Strain into a coupe. Adjust brine to taste. Add cornichon.

30. Poison Apple Martini

Serving: Serves 1 | Prep: | Cook: | Ready in:

Ingredients

- 2 ounces Crown Royal Canadian Whiskey
- 1 ounce Sour Apple Pucker Schnapps
- 2 ounces Cranberry Juice
- 1 ounce Apple Juice

Direction

- Pour whiskey, schnapps and juice into a mixing glass filled with ice
- Use a spoon to stir until the mixture turns ice cold
- Strain into a martini glass and garnish with an apple slice shaped like a half moon
- Place plastic bat (available at any craft store!) in the center of the apple slice
- Enjoy!

31. Pomegranate Citrus Martini (a.k.a. The Floor Flooder)

Serving: Serves 4 | Prep: | Cook: | Ready in:

Ingredients

- 2 Lemons
- 1 Pink Grapefruit
- 8 ounces POM Wonderful juice
- 2 ounces Simple Syrup
- 2-3 ounces Bacardi O (orange rum)

Direction

- Juice the lemons and the grapefruit into a container with measurements on the side. Use a strainer to catch seeds. (It's personal preference as to how much pulp is included in the juice.)

- Add the POM Wonderful and simple syrup to the juice.
- Put ice cubes in a shaker and add the desired amount of rum.
- Pour 4 ounces of the juice mixture into the shaker. Shake vigorously at least 15 times.
- Strain into a chilled martini glass.
- Salude!

32. Pomegranate Martini

Serving: Makes 1 | Prep: | Cook: | Ready in:

Ingredients

- 2 ounces fresh pomegranate seeds
- 2 ounces freshly squeezed orange juice
- 2 ounces Zubrowka Bison Grass Vodka
- 1/2-1 ounces Campari
- 1/2 tablespoon Grenadine
- 1/2 teaspoon Simple syrup
- 1 tablespoon lemon (if you like it a bit sharp)

Direction

- Put the pomegranate seeds in your shaker and muddle them with a muddler or the end of a clean rolling pin. Try to get as much juice out as possible.
- Add the remaining ingredients and half fill the shaker with ice cubes. Shake vigorously.
- Strain into a chilled martini or coupe glass and serve.

33. Pumpkin Pie Martini A Pumpkin Pie In A Glass

Serving: Makes 1 cocktail | Prep: | Cook: | Ready in:

Ingredients

- 2 ounces vodka
- 1 ounce dark rum
- 1 ounce half and half
- 2 tablespoons canned pure pumpkin puree
- 1 ounce maple syrup
- 1/4 teaspoon pumpkin pie spice
- 1/4 teaspoon pure vanilla extract
- Graham crackers
- Cinnamon
- Sugar

Direction

- Smash up the graham crackers, cinnamon and sugar together. Get the rim of your glass wet and dip it into your cinnamon, sugar, cracker mix. PROTIP: use maple syrup on the glass and you'll get extra flavor and sticking power.
- Combine everything else into your cocktail shaker. Shake like a bandit. Pour and strain into your magnificently rimmed martini glass. Garnish with a little bit of grated nutmeg (fresh, naturally).
- NOTE: If you're interested in making your own pumpkin pie spice try, 4 parts cinnamon, 2 parts ginger, 1 part nutmeg, 1 part allspice, 1/2 part cloves.

34. Raspberry Vodka Martini

Serving: Makes one | Prep: | Cook: | Ready in:

Ingredients

- 1.5 oz Raspberry infused vodka
- 1 tsp Trader Joes Agave syrup
- 1.5 oz Sweet vermouth
- 1 Good squeeze fresh lime juice
- Ice
- Optional fres raspberry

Direction

- Chill martini glasses whilst mixing drink

- Place all ingredients in cocktail shaker, shake well with ice
- Strain and serve in ore chilled glasses.
- Optional.... Float fresh raspberry in glass.

35. St. Patrick's Day Emerald Rain Martini

Serving: Makes 1 cocktail | Prep: | Cook: | Ready in:

Ingredients

- 2 ounces Hypnotiq
- 1 1/4 ounces Deep Eddy Vodka
- 1 splash Orange Juice
- Squeeze of Fresh Lime

Direction

- Shake all the ingredients together thoroughly in a shaker with ice. Serve in a chilled cocktail glass and garnish with a lime wheel

36. St. Patrick's Day Martini – Melontini

Serving: Serves 2 | Prep: | Cook: | Ready in:

Ingredients

- 1 cup ice
- 4 ounces vodka
- 3 ounces melon liqueur
- lime for garnish (optional)

Direction

- In a cocktail shaker filled with ice, add vodka and melon liqueur. Shake.
- Strain into a martini glass and serve.

37. Sunset Pomegranate Martini

Serving: Serves 1 | Prep: | Cook: | Ready in:

Ingredients

- 3 ounces Orange Juice
- 2 ounces Pomegranate Juice
- 1 ounce Vodka
- 1 ounce Peach Schnapps
- Pomegranate seeds, for garnish

Direction

- Fill a cocktail shaker halfway with ice and add orange juice, pomegranate juice, vodka and peach schnapps. Shake and strain into a martini glass. Garnish with pomegranate seeds.

38. Tamarind Martinis

Serving: Makes 2 | Prep: | Cook: | Ready in:

Ingredients

- 1 ounce tamarind concentrate
- 4 ounces cold water
- 2 ounces vodka
- 6 tablespoons Tajin (mixture of chili powder and sugar)
- 1 lime, cut into wedges
- ice

Direction

- In a martini shaker add the tamarind concentrate, water, vodka, and ice. Shake until all the ingredients are incorporated.
- Rim a martini glass with lime and dip into the Tajin powder. Pour the martini mixture and enjoy!

39. The Duke's Hotel Vesper Martini

Serving: Serves one | Prep: | Cook: | Ready in:

Ingredients

- 4 dashes Bitters
- 2 tablespoons Lillet Blanc
- 2 shots Potachi Vodka
- 2 shots Berry Bros and Rudd, No 3 Gin
- 1 piece Orange Peel

Direction

- Make sure vodka, gin and martini glass are stored in the freezer. Take out martini glass, add bitters, Lillet, then vodka and finally gin and garnish with orange peel. Serve immediately.

40. The Filthiest Martini

Serving: Makes 1 large cocktail | Prep: | Cook: | Ready in:

Ingredients

- Cucumber Dill Infused Vodka
- A bunch of fresh dill
- 1 large cucumber, chopped
- 1.75 liters vodka, the cheaper the better
- The Cocktail
- 2 ounces Cucumber Dill Infused Vodka
- 1 ounce Vermouth (optional)
- 1 splash Pickle juice

Direction

- Cucumber Dill Infused Vodka
- Add cucumbers and dill to a large sealable container. I used a large mason jar. Add the vodka and let it sit for about 6-7 days, shaking the container once a day.
- Strain cucumbers and dill and enjoy. The leftover vodka should be kept in a cool, dark place and is good for at least a couple months.

- The Cocktail
- In a cocktail shaker combine ingredients with a handful of ice, and pour into a chilled martini glass. Or you can combine ingredients and then pour over ice.
- Garnish with a pickle, or some olives, or both!

41. The Ultimate Chocolate Martini

Serving: Serves 2 | Prep: | Cook: | Ready in:

Ingredients

- 5 tablespoons Absolut Vanilla vodka
- 1/4 cup Godiva chocolate liquor
- 2 tablespoons creme de cacao
- 2 tablespoons frangelico
- 2 tablespoons Bailey's Irish Cream
- chocolate syrup, as needed for garnish
- chocolate shavings, as needed for garnish

Direction

- Be sure to chill the martini glasses you want to use for a few hours in the refrigerator before making the drinks. When you're ready to serve, take out the glasses and decorate them with chocolate syrup. Get some ice into a drink shaker. Add the vodka, chocolate liqueur, crème de cacao, Frangelico, and Irish cream. Give it a good, thorough shake to make sure it is well mixed.
- Pour the mixture from the shaker through a strainer right into the glasses. Top with pretty chocolate shavings and serve immediately! Depending on how big the glasses are and how much you want to fill them, this can make 1-2 martinis. The recipe is easy to double if more is needed. Enjoy!

42. Thyme For A "Grilled" Lemon Martini

Serving: Serves 1-2 (may be doubled) | Prep: | Cook: | Ready in:

Ingredients

- 1 bunch Thyme
- 2 Lemons
- 1 tablespoon Sugar
- 4 ounces Cranberry-infused Vodka
- 2 ounces Amaretto

Direction

- Heat grill to medium high. Place 2 martini glasses in freezer.
- Place Thyme bunch in a small bowl, pour one cup water over herbs, and soak while preparing lemons.
- Cut each lemon into three thick slices. Place sugar on a saucer and swirl to cover bottom of saucer. Press each side of each lemon in the sugar and place on a plate.
- Drain Thyme and shake to remove excess water.
- Grill lemons for one minute on each side. When lemons are ready to turn, place Thyme on grill and cook for up to one minute, turning once; do not burn. Remove lemons and thyme from grill and cool for five minutes.
- Strip Thyme leaves from stem to obtain 1 tablespoon. Place leaves in the bottom of a martini shaker. Press leaves down with a wooden spoon until lightly crushed.
- Squeeze lemons into measuring cup and yield 1/8 cup plus 1 tablespoon lemon juice. Add lemon juice to martini shaker, followed by vodka and Amaretto. Place 1 cup ice cubes in shaker. Shake until chilled.
- Remove martini glasses from freezer. Place a strainer over each glass and pour half of shaker mixture into glass. Garnish with fresh thyme sprig, if desired.

43. Vesper Martini

Serving: Serves 2 | Prep: | Cook: | Ready in:

Ingredients

- 1 1/2 ounces Ketel One vodka
- 1/2 ounce Tanqueray gin
- 1/4 to 1/2 ounces Lillet Blanc
- Lemon peel, for garnish

Direction

- Add all ingredients to a mixing glass, add ice, and stir for 10 seconds. Strain into a coupe and garnish with a lemon peel.

44. Virgin Green Appletini Or Non Alcoholic Green Apple Martini

Serving: Serves 2 | Prep: 0hours15mins | Cook: 0hours10mins | Ready in:

Ingredients

- 2 pieces Green apple
- 1 cup Sugar
- 2 cups Soda water
- 2 pieces Green apple slice

Direction

- First peel both the apple and take out the core.
- In a saucepan, take sugar, water, the peels and the cores of both apple.
- Turn off heat and allow the green apple syrup to cool completely.
- Pour into a martini glass, top with a green apple slice and serve!

45. WHEELS OF FIRE MARTINI
This Wheel's On Fire

Serving: Serves 1 | Prep: | Cook: | Ready in:

Ingredients

- 3 ounces *WHEELS OF FIRE EARL TEA, chilled
- 2 ounces Vodka
- 3 Pimiento olives speared

Direction

- *Brew I cup, (8-10 oz.) *WHEELS OF FIRE EARL TEA, 3-4 minutes, chill. Makes 2-4 drinks. (Use WHEELS OF FIRE TEA for Molotov cocktail heat)
- Directions: Shake tea, and vodka with ice and strain into chilled martini glass. Add olives.

46. Wicked Witch Martini

Serving: Serves 2 | Prep: | Cook: | Ready in:

Ingredients

- 6 ounces vodka
- 1 ounce dry vermouth
- 1 tablespoon olive juice
- 1 cup cracked ice
- 2 green stuffed olives
- 2 eyeballs, preferably fake

Direction

- Decorate two martini glasses with spiders and cobwebs and place them in the refrigerator to chill.
- Combine the vodka, vermouth, olive juice, and ice in a cocktail shaker. Shake until well chilled, about 20 to 30 seconds. Strain the mixture into the chilled glasses, add an olive and an eyeball to each glass, and serve.

47. Wild Blueberry Martini

Serving: Serves 2 | Prep: | Cook: | Ready in:

Ingredients

- 2 tablespoons wild blueberry spread
- 4 ounces vodka
- lots of ice

Direction

- Place your martini glasses in the freezer for about 20 minutes before you make your martinis.
- Place the ice into your martini shaker. Add the blueberry spread (I use St. Dalfour, just make sure you stir it well, as the blueberries tend to be on the top) and the vodka.
- Cover and shake well. Pour into your ice cold martini glasses making sure you spoon in the blueberries...delicious treat at the end. Serve immediately.

48. Winter Grilled Lobster Martinis

Serving: Serves 8 | Prep: | Cook: | Ready in:

Ingredients

- Lobster
- 3 pounds Maine Lobsters
- Good Extra Virgin Olive Oil
- Pinch Sea Salt
- 8 Fresh Lemongrass Stalks (optional)
- 2 Grapefruits Juiced
- Sun Jus Vinaigrette
- 3 Ripe Tomatoes Diced
- 1 Cucumber Seeded & Diced
- 1 Red Bell Pepper Diced
- 1 Yellow Bell Pepper Diced
- 1/2 Medium Vidalia Onion Diced
- 1 bunch Cilantro Chopped

- 3 tablespoons Seasoned Rice Wine Vinegar
- 6 tablespoons Good Olive Oil
- 1 Small Jalapeno, Seeded & Minced

Direction

- For Vinaigrette: Combine all ingredients, adding Jalapeno to taste. Let sit at room temperature approximately 4 hours to let flavors blend.
- Split each lobster and clean, keeping meat in the shell. Season salt and freshly ground pepper. Marinate lobsters in olive oil and grapefruit juice for one hour. Drain and discard marinade. Grill lobsters over hot coals or preheated gas grill for approximately 5 minutes. DO NOT OVERCOOK. Remove lobster meat from shells, rough chop and place in martini glasses. Top with vinaigrette and garnish with swizzle stick of lemongrass or leaf of radicchio.
- Optional Modifications: Sprinkle 2 Tbs. of flavored (orange, cranberry or lemon) or plain vodka over each martini.

49. YUZU MARTINI

Serving: Serves 1 | Prep: | Cook: | Ready in:

Ingredients

- 50 milliliters Cape North Vodka
- 1 milliliter Grand Marnier
- 10 milliliters Lemon Juice
- 15 milliliters Sugar
- 4 dashes Yuzu Juice
- 1 dash Orange Bitter

Direction

- Shaken and double strain into chilled Martini glass

50. Yotam Ottolenghi And Lukasz Rafacz's Sumac Martini

Serving: Serves 2 | Prep: | Cook: | Ready in:

Ingredients

- For the sumac-infused vodka:
- 3 tablespoons sumac
- 1 bottle (750 ml) of high-quality vodka
- For the sumac martini:
- 2 ounces (60 ml) sumac-infused vodka
- 1 1/4 ounces (40 ml) Velvet Falernum liqueur
- 1 3/4 ounces (50 ml) lime juice
- 1 1/4 ounces (40 ml) pomegranate juice
- a few pinches sumac, to garnish

Direction

- To make the infused vodka, place the sumac in a large glass or ceramic bowl and pour over the vodka. Cover and set aside for 2 hours, stirring from time to time, then strain back into the bottle through a fine-mesh or muslin-lined sieve.
- When ready to serve, place all the ingredients in a shaker with some cubed ice. Shake really hard for 10 to 15 seconds, then double-strain (through a strainer and into a fine-mesh sieve) into two chilled glasses. Serve at once, with a sprinkle of sumac on top.

Index

Conclusion

Thank you again for downloading this book!

I hope you enjoyed reading about my book!

If you enjoyed this book, please take the time to share your thoughts and post a review on Amazon. It'd be greatly appreciated!

Write me an honest review about the book – I truly value your opinion and thoughts and I will incorporate them into my next book, which is already underway.

Thank you!

If you have any questions, **feel free to contact at:** *author@syruprecipes.com*

Linda Davis

syruprecipes.com

Your Note

Your Note

Your Note

Your Note

Your Note

Printed in Great Britain
by Amazon